MONEY

AND

MANNERISM

Becoming the great steward of Money, you were meant to be.

MAXINE GORDON

ISBN 979-8-9988516-1-2 (Hardcover)
ISBN 979-8-9988516-4-3 (Paperback)
ISBN 979-8-9988516-2-9 (eBook)

Author can be contacted via: prophetmax@yahoo.com

Printed in the United States of America

Ayn Rand quote: *"Money is a tool. It will take you wherever you wish, but it will not replace you as the driver. It will give you the means for the satisfaction of your desires, but it will not provide you with desires."*

Epictetus quote: *"Wealth consists not in having great possessions, but in having few wants."*

Table of Contents

MONEY

MANNERISM

Acknowledgments

I thank the Holy Spirit for His inspiration as He guided me in understanding the true meaning of money/currency.

I dedicate this book first to my immediate family; my husband Bishop Gordon and our four beautiful children.

To those who stood with me in prayer, trusting and believing God's Word, may this book catapult you into a new regime of the proper usage of money.

Thanks to everyone who will be reading and receiving a mind and heart transformation.

Foreword

By Dr. Delroy Fray, MBBS (U.W.I) FRCS (Glasg.) FACS
Consultant Surgeon
Clinical Coordinator WRHA

It has been an absolute pleasure reading this book. The concepts and illustrations presented are firmly grounded in biblical truths, making it clear that this work was inspired by God.

From the very first page, I was captivated; unable to put it down until I had read it in its entirety. The message is both powerful and transformative, offering profound insights that resonate deeply with the Christian journey.

As believers, we can all identify with the principles shared in this book and strive to apply them in our daily walk with Christ. It serves as a guiding light, reminding us of the power of faith, obedience, and spiritual growth. The wisdom contained within these pages has the potential to inspire change, strengthen our relationship with God, and deepen our understanding of His purpose for our lives.

I extend my heartfelt congratulations to Prophetess Gordon for this incredible work. May God continue to use you mightily for His kingdom, anointing and equipping you to touch lives and spread His word.

Foreword

I have read through the book and I find it very practical. Very instructive with biblical references.

I believe the principles in it, if applied by the reader, will be very useful in their financial life. Especially to those in the body of Christ where we don't speak about money much, except when it comes to tithes and offering, and sowing seeds.

So I think the work is a good work, and they need to work.

It will be a blessing to many.

Speak life.

Bishop John Cline

New Life Baptist Church (BVI)

Preface

If you are a mundane kind of person who exhibits a dull and lack of excitement lifestyle, obviously you probably would be deemed to society as one that is frugal with spending. But not necessarily true! Money doesn't bring you into a happy space until you become happy with yourself, your core values, who you really are and were meant to be, accepting you, believing in you, and becoming a better version of yourself. Then, when accommodating money, you will be able to navigate well through understanding how best to use it.

It is with great exuberance and drive to be able to cease every opportunity to thrive, succeed, and be able to take care of your money matters. It literally brings your heart into a settled place. How wonderful the feeling of continuous accomplishments!

Having said that, the knowledge of seeking to acquire it honestly and in abundance is pretty normal. The desire to succeed is inevitable. Laying a proper foundation with money enables the trajectory of your financial goals and will be pleasing to the principles of God and the laws of society.

Money can become incapacitated (deprived of its strength and power) to be properly navigated and managed because of senseless ideas, wrong directions and wrong desires.

I am cognizant of the fact that money does not appear by "abracadabra" (simply magic). It is birthed through inheritance, hard work, principle, knowledge and wisdom to properly handle and maintain it.

This book was destined to help capture the true essence and importance of having the right heart posture, motives and desires towards money. It points you to the Do's and Don'ts that will clear the path for handling and cleverly mastering the art of it.

You will receive biblical references, scriptures, as well as experiences to enlighten your path to succeed. This book will allow you to take key notes to avoid simple actions that can cause big problems with your money matters.

Often times anxiety sets in, but carefully navigating your way through this book will keep your adrenaline in the correct mode. This book will teach you how to build on your figures and enhance those beautiful goals and dreams that are long awaited. You will pivot with purpose!

Let the journey begin!

MONEY

> “ *I laid down the love for money,*
> *and watch God save,*
> *heal and deliver lives,*
> *while he blessed us.*

What is Money?

Money is a current medium of exchange whether cash or bank note. Other names to describe money are bucks, dough, and funds. Money basically runs the world. The Greek meaning for money is mammon; it is seen as 'life'. Jesus quoted this scripture in **John 15:13 - "Greater love hath no man than this, that a man lay down his life for his friends." It also said in Matthew 6:24 -"No man can serve two masters: for either he will hate the one, and love the other; or else he will hold to the one, and despise the other. Ye cannot serve God and mammon."** In other words, money is a master that must not be served; we must lay it down in our hearts and serve God only. Money should instead be mastered by us.

I used to work with one of the largest banks in our country, and it was truly exciting. Professionally attiring day to day and being into what I called a prestigious type of job, thoughts of owning my own home in my twenties, my car and dreams of being able to travel the world captivated the very core of my being. A promotion came about for me and before I could celebrate, suddenly the door shut right in my face. I was absolutely devastated. I cried my eyes out for days, because not only was the promotion not available, but I was also released from the job.

I just could not wrap my head around it then. I worked well and got commendations. The last day of crying about it, God visited me! This was his question **"will you lay down your life for me?"** This question was asked twice. I answered, **"Lord I am not ready to die." He said, "I am not talking about your physical body, I am talking about money!"** He continued, **"you forgot that I told you before I opened that door at the bank, that you would not be there for long, because I ordained you to do full-time Ministry for me. When I close a door, no man can open it!"**

I cried breathlessly before him. I released the burden of what I had considered a loss, and I heeded the call of Ministry. I am now twenty-nine years in ministry with my husband. God has been good! I laid down the love for money and watched God save, heal, and deliver lives while he provided and blessed us. Glory to the mighty name of Jesus Christ.

1 Timothy 6:10 - "The love of money is the root of all evil", that is, when you have an intense feeling and deep attraction for it. We should love God with all our hearts, souls and minds, and our neighbour as ourselves. There is absolutely no way that our endearment should be geared towards money.

> “*This shows how much God as the creator of all things,*
>
> *and the manager of all currencies,*
>
> *stock in heaven is waiting to release on earth.*

Money Matters

Ecclesiastes 10:19 - "Money answereth all things". Money is classified as a tool, that has usage to all things. It is a gift from God (a blessing, a sign). It is a sure sign that God will make provision that would be needed.

I can remember vividly an encounter I had with God. I saw the bank of heaven open. There were crazy stockpiles of money. I could only see the backside of God as he was commanding his angels to distribute accordingly to the saints. It was quite breathtaking and prodigious (great in extent). I suddenly hoped for my name to be called. What an incredible sight it was to behold!

This shows how much more God, as the creator of all things and the manager of all currencies stocked in heaven, is waiting to release in the earth. It is very important to pay attention to money, it's also vital to approach it from an accurate perspective. I remembered walking pass coins spilled on the floor by my children, and sometimes it was hard to keep bending. In a subtle manner the thought was that these few coins are nothing, but that is how we can operate with naivety!

One day I could recall the voice of renowned Evangelist- Joyce Meyers saying, how she used to ignore coins on the floor, and God spoke to her, told her that one day he will make her rich. Something jolted in me and I said to myself, "Maxine, you are not the slightest near Joyce (where finances are concerned) and you are ignoring coins. Since then, I started a coin drive in my home. I had this big plastic jar, and it was almost full, when our home was burglarized and the coins were stolen. Unfortunately, it was sad, but at least I obeyed the principle and still do to this day.

The foundational concept of the bible, revealed about money, is that we should put our trust in God rather than money. **Matthew 6:21 – "For where your treasure is, there will your heart be also."** This basically means, if one's treasure is on earth, one's heart and attention will also be on earthly materials. It is an implicit warning to all of us.

> *It is necessary to have currency,*
> *that will move and flow,*
> *to accomplish what is necessary to be done.*
> *The power to create wealth is to create,*
> *obtain, assimilate or possess wealth.*

The Relevance of Money

Proverbs 13:22 - "Good people leave an inheritance to their grandchildren, but the sinner's wealth passes to the godly." (NLT). "…the wealth of the sinner is laid up for the just." (KJV)

A good man's estate lasts when he leaves an inheritance for his children. It is a part of the praise that he is thoughtful for posterity, that he doesn't 'layout' only for himself. The man that does this would be considered wise, prudent and frugal. In manifesting these character traits, by being good and doing good, by honoring the Lord with his substance and spending it in his service, ties it to his prosperity.

The book of **Malachi 3:10** tells us to bring all the tithes into the storehouse and verse eight asks the question, **"Will a man rob God? Yet ye have robbed me. … In tithes and offerings."** This means God requires the tenth. By tithing, we are giving back to our creator, who is quite considerable. This tenth rightly belongs to him.

Tithing is seen as a religious duty. Its roots, dating back to Abraham tithing to Melchizedek, is used to support priesthood and religious institutions. In the book of Malachi chapter 3, God gave a promise that those who tithe he will open the windows of heaven and pour out his blessings on them. Tithing therefore is an act of worship unto God, to honor and reverence Him with our substance. It is just as relevant now, as it was in those days.

God sees you withholding your tithe as robbing Him. **Malachi 3:9** says **"Ye are cursed with a curse."** This means you are cursed with a curse that he has allowed (scarcity, isolation, financial debt and limitation to your blessing) instead of abundant life. Jesus said, 'I come to give you life and life more abundantly' (**John 10:10**); Money is included too! With such a curse, it is as if there would be a pause on your life.

This command is serious; therefore, it should be taken seriously. Bring it into the house, depositing, so there will be meat (prey and food). Meat (**Mal. 3:10**) in this case also represents affluence, strength and provision for the work. It's also blessings, pouring out, mercy and everything that would come to strengthen the work of God and the work of your life. Tithing also goes with an exemplary lifestyle, hunger for righteousness, and holiness to become holy as Christ is holy.

Not every child of God accepts the revelation of tithing given through God's word. Verse 10 of that same passage of scripture says, **"[look] if I will not open you the windows of heaven, and pour you out a blessing, that there shall not be room enough to receive it." (Mal. 3:10)**

The windows of heaven here, are not just referring to financial blessings. Your life will increase, you will grow in the things of God. Your God-given abilities, talents and gifts will increase. He said you will not have enough room - physical and spiritual. How powerful is the understanding of tithing!

God will fight the devil on your behalf. Verse 11 says **"I will rebuke the devourer".** That is anything (pest or pestilence) that will hinder your harvest, or anything else that comes to devour. God will release a strong expression of disapproval (stern and sharp discipline) to the enemy of your crop (that ferocious eater that feeds and eats up your finances, your health, your ministry, and your marriage). The enemy that has been taking away your nourishment. The fruit of your labor will not fail. Your vine in your field will produce fruit. (**Duet. 28:8**) Whatsoever you put your hands to, will prosper. Your crop will unleash abundance. God will manifest his copiousness.

This is the covenant that God made with us if we obey His word. They will see the blessing of God on you. It will be known and visible. You will be talked about. A delightsome land you will be-pleasures of contentment to the mind and senses.

God said it is he that gives the power to create wealth (***Duet. 8:18***). It's necessary to have currency that will move, and flow, to do and accomplish what is necessary to be done. The power to create wealth is to create, obtain, assimilate or possess wealth. Power is available coupled with wisdom. **Ecclesiastes 10:10 - "Wisdom is profitable to direct."**

On three occasions God confronted me with a sharp rebuke concerning my tithes. My tithe lingered for a while before entering the tithe basket at my church. In other words, I delayed. God spoke to me clearly and said to me **"Oh you have robbed me in your tithes and offerings."** I believed He saw that the delay would eventually cause me to dip into the tithe for other reasons. I immediately moved and put my tithe in. On the second occasion, I gave it to someone who delayed the process. When God's voice came back the third time, I had the tithe sitting in the bank and I heard God say to me clearly, **"Give me my money."** That caused me to move with speed, as I wanted to reverence God and to live under an 'open heaven.'

Note, everyone might not have had my experience, but truly I am grateful to God for helping me to give him willingly His portion.

Your tithe and offering sets the trajectory for funding the work of God and for your future great blessing; not just for you, but for you and your children. **Psalm 115:14** says, **"The Lord shall increase you more and more, you and your children."** We ought to prove Him with the truth. If you don't love money, then you will give Him His portion. Let's do it, for the work of the Lord!

> *Earth's resources come from*
> *God's dynasty in heaven.*
> *That the Glory cannot be shared*
> *with no man.*

Don't Love It

Whosoever loves it never has enough (**Ecc. 5:10**). Solomon cuts right to the heart of the matter, that the love of money leaves you wanting more and more. One will do just about anything to have it (break protocols, tell a lie, take a life, put someone else above, break a back). If we love it, we do whatever it calls for! It is the root of all evil (wickedness, viciousness, iniquitousness).

Many lives have been scoffed out and many are in prison for the love of it. **Proverbs 13:11** tells us that dishonest moves, vanity will never last. It will be vaporized! Only those who work for it shall increase. It is why God's word says that by the sweat of a man's brow, he shall eat bread (**Gen. 3:19**).

It is also known as the root/foundation of all evil (**1 Timothy 6:10**). From the moment the love of money comes into a life, one can never be the same. It begins to control and manipulate you because God would be on the back burner in you. Suddenly you would be hearing the voice of money; a voice that would say to you 'If you love me you can't serve God; I will take the place of God in your life.'

Your life will come to nothing if you listen to the voice of money that wants you to serve it! The outcome of loving it and becoming a slave to it can become such a tumultuous reign.

We look at the story of Jesus, when Judas sold him out for thirty pieces of silver (***Matt. 26:15***). Judas was with Jesus all the time. He was the treasurer; but Satan had entered his heart.

The truth is money can be enticing to the mind. It becomes so attractive to the eye. If Judas needed money, he could have asked Jesus. But prophecy had to be fulfilled! **Zechariah 11:13 - "And the LORD said to me, "Throw it to the potter" - the handsome price at which they valued me! So I took the thirty pieces of silver and threw them to the potter at the house of the LORD."**

Judas did not value money and so he did not value the King of kings. The money became 'blood money' that was given to betray a life. How malevolent was Judas, ignoramus (foolish and stupid) along with it. The lust of the eye was evident in this case (**1 John 2:16**) and is an inherent temptation, snare, and pitfall of all that is in and of the world. So also, is the pride of life. How God hates pride! It was pride that had Satan and a third of his angels kicked out of heaven.

The fact that Satan wanted to be in charge, he coveted what was in heaven (the splendor, the magnificence, the grandeur of God's riches). Remember in heaven Satan used to walk on stones of fire. All the riches and all the glory were visible to the eyes. He had begun to fall heavily in love with what could only belong to God.

Earth's resources come from God's dynasty in heaven. That glory cannot be shared with no man.

Would we recognize that no matter how a human being loves money to the moon and back, if he dies tomorrow, he has to leave it all here on earth? **Matthew 6:19-21 – "Lay not up for yourself treasures upon earth, where moth and rust doth corrupt, where thieves break through and steal: But lay up for yourselves treasures in heaven, where neither moth or rust doth corrupt, and where thieves do not break through nor steal: For where your treasure is, there will your heart be also."**

Our top priorities should be God, not money. No wonder Jesus said, **Philippians 4:6-7 NKJV - "Be anxious for nothing…".** Anxious in the Greek means to be restless, weary, or worrisome; Agog (impatient or ongoing impatience). **"...but in everything by prayer and supplication, with thanksgiving, let your requests be made known to God; and the peace of God, which surpasses all understanding, will guard your hearts and minds through Christ Jesus."**

Satan wants you to beg, borrow or steal. Nothing is wrong with begging or borrowing, but from who? If you are in a good position to, God wants us to be lenders and not borrowers, givers and not beggars (**Duet. 15:6**). The aim of Satan is to corrupt the seed of money because he wasn't able to be in charge. So, he makes people die for it, cut up one another for it, or bury some alive for it. He definitely corrupted the seed. Scripture says in (**Gen. 3:15**) that the seed of the woman shall bruise his head. Jesus crushed the head of the serpent! Jesus came to make all things new, even though it was corrupted through one man Adam. Through one man sin entered the world (**Rom. 5:12**).

What do you think would have happened to Cain if God did not expose him? He would have taken what was his brother's after he had killed him. He was jealous of what would have been a better sacrifice than his. We see families die for their own hard earnings, we see extortionists, we see money being paid to either protect or expunge others. As long as people are paid, they are satisfied. The world is in an upheaval for the love of money and power.

"We have to watch closely to avoid these types of evil from entering the mind.

Don't Waste It!

I remember a dream I had, where I saw this married man with holes in his pocket; Money was leaking from it. I sought the Lord for the interpretation, and he showed me that the married man was committing adultery, and a curse came upon his money. He was not able to complete his goals, dreams and visions for himself and his family because of his selfishness, greed and prideful lifestyle.

It is quite sad that a man would do that to his family and leave them in lack and suffering. Deliverance and the breakage of soul ties is needed to break this curse cycle, so that the financial and ceremonial agreement in marriage can be regained.

How corrupted the love of money can become, that a man or a woman is willing to throw away the peace, protection, and the vital care of a family for lust of the eyes, lust of the flesh and the pride of life. It's used to defame God's blessing on earth. The love and greed for it has absolutely damaged many marriages, families and good relationships. Money for sex has become the order of the day. Money to keep quiet has been the icing on the cake, figuratively speaking. The disrespect for it has ransacked, raped, and sabotaged good marriages by senseless, self-centered and malevolent behavior.

The Jamaican slang, 'sugar daddies' and 'sugar mommas' simply means they release money when the act is executed, to cover tracks, and for bribe. Read in the scripture **Proverb 6:26**, which tells us that a prostitute will treat you like a loaf of bread, and a woman who takes part in adultery will cost you your life. We ought to watch closely to avoid these types of evil from entering the mind. The quickest way for a man or woman to ruin their self is having sex outside of marriage. This is where character and reputation are destroyed. God help us!

Certain types of distribution for money are made across the borders, society, institutions, including the church. A woman would rather a family become unhappy and in turmoil to satisfy greed, jealousy and lust. It is very prevalent among the young also. The body of Christ has to arise and pray. Too many families are bleeding, even ministries and businesses. Forgiveness and deliverance is a must!

Scripture does not say that we should take God's Grace for granted, rather we must be aware that the consequences are the hard parts to endure. But God! Much prayers and genuine repentance, 'turning from' our wrongs, is of true essence.

The plan of Satan is to corrupt all seeds. Money is also defined as a seed. The misconception of money has left many becoming bewildered, in a state of shock and perplexity. This blessing that God has created, has malfunctioned in the hand of those who do not respect it!

Scripture quotes in **Psalms 28:1-4 - "Unto thee will I cry, O Lord my rock; be not silent to me: lest, if thou be silent to me, I become like them that go down into the pit. Hear the voice of my supplications, when I cry unto thee, when I lift up my hands toward thy holy oracle. Draw me not away with the wicked..."**

Money has taken an ugly form because of the type of hearts. It is not a blessing but a curse. It has become blood money, witchcraft money, sex money, plot to kill money, and the list goes on.

Allow me to share a poem God gave me about money...

Money

Money, you are a good thing,

But to love you, this race I won't win.

The love for you brings devastation,

To cherish you, causes marital separation.

To live for you breaks family relation.

Oh Money!

You are a good thing,

But what man has made you to be, causes many to be killed.

To live for you, Christ I won't gain,

To worship you, I would only live in pain,

And God's blessings I will not attain.

Yes! Money you are needed, but Jesus Christ must be exalted.

From the Book:

'Pure Gems of Glory' by Maxine J. Gordon

There are so many blessings that comes to a man when he fears the Lord. His wife and family will be tremendously blessed. Psalm 128:3 NLT says, "Your wife will be like a fruitful grapevine, flourishing within your home. Your children will be like vigorous young olive trees as they sit around your table." Therefore, a man in his power has to do everything possible for the restitution and restoration of the family, whilst the anatomy of those caught in the web of disgrace, shame and embarrassment are replaced with healing by God's grace.

Pray this prayer -

Lord your word says money answereth all things and it's not intended to mix with sin. Help man's resources to be navigated by wisdom and integrity, so that their labor will not be in vain and the fruit will be visible. I pray for protection over the bread winners. Allow them to manifest frugality with understanding, and let your word be the basis on which they build their financial goals and dreams. I cancel every satanic attack against marriages and money in Jesus' mighty name. I DECLARE THAT THEY WILL PROSPER AND BE IN GOOD HEALTH, EVEN AS THEIR SOUL PROSPERS (**3 John 2**)

“It’s nonsensical for us to just keep falling into deeper debt, and not applying both natural and spiritual principles, Don’t give out of compulsion.

The Spendthrift Mentality

Jane once told me how miserable she was feeling, and disappointed in herself. I asked her what was going on. She remarked that she had ten thousand US dollars in debt that she could not afford to pay back. This was what happened to Jane. She wanted to help everyone out of "not enough." She literally found herself giving away money, as if it grew on a tree. Jane had bills piling up! And at almost every approach, she gave.

Note! You cannot help someone if you don't have the means to help. I know some of us have a giving heart, but God help us to use wisdom. Jane went bankrupt. A thing as a credit card, is always the bank's money. Should you offer to appease someone, know exactly how you are going to repay. It's nonsensical for us to just keep falling deeper into debt and not applying both natural and spiritual principles. Don't give out of compulsion. Don't stretch yourself more than you can. Avoid the consequences of embarrassment and shame. Pivot well!

"There is treasure to be desired
and oil in the dwelling of the wise;
But a foolish man spendeth it up."

Proverbs 21:20

Hoarding

Let's take a look at hoarding- I would classify hoarding to an extent as, storing up things unnecessarily that's not being used. It is a strong passion and drive to just accumulate lots of things constantly.

Debra is a hoarder who spends frivolously without realizing that she is squandering and wasting. She was quite materialistic and was overly concerned about her possessions, which had gotten her into such dilemma. Debra's mental state needed serious adjustments. She became out of control. A hoarder will never be able to focus on a specific goal or dream. This is definitely a stronghold in her mental space that needs pulling down through prayers; and possibly cognitive behavioral therapy will be needed.

Debra wasted so much money and was in need of so much help.

Hoarding does not make one an image, but a fool. **Proverbs 21:20 - "There is treasure to be desired and oil in the dwelling of the wise; But a foolish man spendeth it up."**

There is an old-time proverb that says - A fool and their money shall soon depart.

I was once a Hoarder of shoes, because I loved it so much, but I was delivered. Glory to Jesus!

❝*Riches should not cause us to have confidence in the flesh, but in God. It is Him who gives the power for it.*

The Boastful Rich

Jeremiah 9:23-24 - "Thus saith the LORD, let not the wise man glory in his wisdom, neither let the mighty man glory in his might, let not the rich man glory in his riches: But let him that glorieth glory in this, that he understandeth and knoweth me, that I am the LORD which exercise lovingkindness, judgment, and righteousness, in the earth: for in these things I delight, saith the LORD."

In this world of sin and sorrow, ending soon in death and judgment, how foolish for men to glory in their knowledge, health, strength and riches, or anything that leads under the dominion of sin and the wrath of God. Riches should not cause us to have confidence in the flesh but in God. It is God who gives the power for it; therefore, he should get all the glory out of it. HALLELUJAH!

I had the privilege some years ago to be invited along with my children by a rich dude to his house, who was also a Motivational Speaker. I hesitated because I could hear the boastfulness in his tone about his possessions. I eventually went and his house was beautiful, which I told him. He then introduced me to his wife, who I could not understand to this day.

They took us to the room where we'd be staying, as I had decided we would have only been there for one night. Every time this man would open his mouth, it was about his possessions. I had begun to feel annoyed. We weren't there for it, we weren't interested in it. We were invited for a day! Let us relax.

Everything was rigid. His wife would time us when to get to pool and when to get out. Literally, she would clap her hands as if we were her children. Of course, by the grace of God I knew how to behave myself wisely and professionally. I could not wait for 24 hours to go by. The drama continued when night came, and she clapped those hands again to tell us it's bedtime and lights out! I swallowed my saliva and declared that my children and I would have a goodnight sleep. Morning came and we prepared ourselves for the day. We were excited because we were leaving. We were summoned to the breakfast table, where we gave thanks and ate. I showed gratitude to the couple and as we were leaving, they packed up leftovers (which they also ate from) to give to us. This time the line was crossed the more. My children and I refused such gift. We went on our way, and I had to comfort them as the bigger person. Lessons to be learned!

MANNERISM

> *We have to develop 'that' mannerism for money*
>
> *and also realize that we ought to treat it well.*

Mannerism

Mannerism is deemed as a habitual gesture or affectation (distinctive quality or style). God has given me the title of this book with the knowledge of how we should utilize money with much quality and respect. Note that mannerism has a negative side that can be played out in many ways, by bad habitual patterns. For example, coughing without covering your mouth, not knowing how to say, “Good Morning”, “Excuse me”, and the list goes on.

As human beings we should manifest mannerism to money as well; Respect it! It should not be used for filthy gain. **Ecclesiastes 7:12 - “Wisdom is a defence, and money is a defence: but the excellency of knowledge is, that wisdom giveth life to them that have it.”** I find that people who do not have wisdom cannot and will not respect money for what it is. (**Acts 8:18-20**) Simon the sorcerer lacked so much mannerism for money that he thought he could buy God’s gifts with it. The disciples were so disgruntled, that Peter said to him in verse 20, **“thy money perish with thee...”**. Again, what you don’t respect, you will no longer attract.

We therefore have to develop that mannerism for money and also realize that we ought to treat it well in return so that it will dwell with us in the most wise and peaceful way.

Another way to manifest money mannerisms is the principle that when you borrow, you pay back. (**Exo. 22:14**) If anyone borrows, it must be paid back in full; restitution must be made. Oftentimes, even among the body of Christ, we borrow and then harbor offense when it's time to pay back. **Psalms 37:21 ESV - "The wicked borrows but does not pay back, but the righteous is generous and gives."** I find that it's these kinds of folks are usually the meanest; they do not give or share!

"If you lend money to one of my people
among you who is needy,
do not treat it like a business deal;
charge no interest."

Exodus 22:25 NIV

Don't Over Charge

Exodus 22:25 - "If thou lend money to any of my people that is poor by thee, thou shalt not be to him as an usurer, neither shalt thou lay upon him usury."

The scripture is clearly stating that if you lend the poor money, don't seek to get interest on your returns. This is not pleasing to God. Oftentimes they can barely pay you back. We should be satisfied with the return of the amount that was loaned.

Those who refuse to obey honest principles will ruin themselves. We should show respect to others. Displaying integrity and self-awareness.

“

The man who applies himself diligently to his job, will have wealth.

But a sluggard will be poor.

Work For It

Do honest work for it. It's a sign that you have money mannerism. **Proverbs 10:4 NIV - "Lazy hands make for poverty."** Poor or rich the choice is yours to make today, tomorrow and the next day. The man who applies himself diligently to his job will have wealth, but a slacker or sluggard will be poor. Success requires energy, focus and persistent efforts. Get to work now! Sluggards usually put their hands in their pockets, and it is folded across the chest. **Proverbs 19:24 - "A slothful man hideth his hand in his bosom, and will not so much as bring it to his mouth again."** There is no respect for working hard for it! The hand is a figure of speech (metaphorically speaking), meaning no provision will enter the mouth.

Respect is due to money.

“It is more sensible (and fair)

to let the worker have his or her fair portion,

to fulfill their needs.

Do Not Muzzle The Ox

It is imperative that we understand this scripture in its deepest form. (**1 Timothy 5:15**) Do not muzzle (be stingy, or have close fists), while those who tread the corn/work for their honest wage is denied of it. If we truly manifest that respect, we will respect others enough to give them a fair wage. Money is truly currency that flows for great purposes and reasons. **Leviticus 19:13 - "Thou shall not defraud thy neighbour, neither rob him: the wages of him that is hired shall not abide with thee all night until morning."**

The oppression of money in the workplace and in society is real. This scripture is referring, more so, to folks who depend on their wages 100%. Sometimes bosses would spitefully delay payment when they could have easily released what is no longer theirs. This right here is wickedness! They will be accountable to God. I remembered on two occasions, I had delayed paying two persons who had done jobs for me and God visited me. Even though I considered it not to be on purpose. His words to me were from 1 Corinthians 9:9, Do not muzzle the ox that treads the corn. It means the Ox which signifies a human cannot replenish the strength while it works. It is more sensible (and fair) to let the worker have his or her fair portion to fulfill their needs.

Integrity of words and needs are highly important.

Annanias and Sapphira were two church criminals. They lied to the Apostle (**Acts 5:1-11**). They sold land and kept the bulk of the sum for themselves. This had resulted in both of them losing their lives. They lied in the presence of Holy Spirit. These apostles were men full of the spirit of God and could discern their works. May this grace return to the churches to glorify God's righteousness and justice.

I had one visitation from God concerning a pastor and his wife. At the time of the visitation, I was minding my business and working with my hands (**1 Thes 4:11**). He called them Annanias and Sapphira. I was actually stunned, because in no way had I seen them as such. Trying to avoid not getting ahead of myself, I prayed about it and asked God to bring clarity. God gave me the opportunity to see it played out before my eyes. Then I asked God for His mercy on their behalf. I don't know if they had repented, but that's between them and God.

Saints we should truly pray that the dreaded fear of God re-enters the church of Jesus Christ. Our crassness is too much in the face of God for far too long. We do things without even thinking about how it would affect others, our deity and purpose. God is most gracious and compassionate, slow to anger and plenteous in mercies (**Psalms 103:8**). He also has other sides to him. He is a man of war (**Ex. 15:3**), he is great and terrible (**Neh. 1:5**), and he is a consuming fire (**Heb. 12:29**). God will not compromise with sin. He still judges, lest we think we stand - then we fall. I even more developed this pattern of speech to my every day walk, as God's mercies are on my life. **Hebrews 10:31 NIV - "It is a dreadful thing to fall into the hands of the living God". Repent, and come quickly!**

If while reading this chapter you feel convicted of lacking integrity and honesty, go to God, confess, and receive forgiveness.

> *Money has a platform on earth as it is in heaven.*

Avoid the Disease

Because of human's owns perspective on Money. It can be viewed as an infectious disease. Why? Simply because of handlings. Money has a platform on earth, and it is why the prayer says, **"Give us this day our daily bread" (Matthew 6:11)**. Earth's resources are governed by heaven. The disease clearly is to love it, but the healing is to use it for the glory of God's name.

> *Think before you leap.*
>
> *Develop a plan of action.*

Wise Budgeting

There is an old proverb that says, **"If you want it all, you will lose it all." (Proverbs 13:16**) A wise man thinks ahead, a fool doesn't, and even brags about it. These are great words of King Solomon, that a prudent person weighs options carefully before acting. Think before you leap. Develop a plan of action.

These are great ways to appropriate funds:

1. Tithing: **Malachi 3:10 - "Bring ye all the tithes into the storehouse, that there may be meat in mine house."**

2. Meet Family Needs: **1 Timothy 5:8 - "But if any provide not for his own, and specially for those of his own house, he hath denied the faith, and is worse than an infidel."**

3. Keep cash flow positively: **Deuteronomy 8:18 – "But thou shalt remember the LORD thy God: for it is he that giveth thee power to get wealth, …"**

4. Save for the future: **Proverbs 21:20 – "There is treasure to be desired and oil in the dwelling of the wise; but a foolish man spendeth it up."**

5. Interest in your goals, dreams and visions: **Jeremiah 29:11 - "For I know the thoughts that I think toward you, saith the LORD, thoughts of peace, and not of evil, to give you an expected end."** Even through a long wait.

6. Debt Free: **Romans 13:8 - "Owe no man any thing, but to love one another: for he that loveth another has fulfilled the law."**

7. Help those in need: **Hebrews 13:16 - "But to do good and to communicate forget not: for with such sacrifices God is well pleased." Luke 6:30 – "Give to every man that asketh of thee; and of him that taketh away thy goods ask them not again."**

In a nutshell - SAVE SOME, SOW SOME, SPEND SOME, SACRIFICE SOME

Proverbs 28:27 – "He that giveth unto the poor shall not lack: but he that hideth his eyes shall have many a curse."

Proverbs 21:26 – "He coveteth greedily all the day long: but the righteous giveth and spareth not."

Mark 12:41-44 – "And Jesus sat over against the treasury, and beheld how the people cast money into the treasury: and many that were rich cast in much. And there came a certain poor widow, and she threw in two mites, which make a farthing. And he called unto him his disciples, and saith unto them, Verily I say unto you, That this poor widow hath cast more in, than all they which have cast into the treasury: For all they did cast in of their abundance; but she of her want did cast in all that she had, even all her living."

8. Do good and rewarding investments: **Matthew 25:14-30** – (Parable of the Talent)

> *"The only way you can serve God*
> *and give true worship,*
> *is to remove the love of wealth*
> *from our hearts and let Jesus in.*

Wealth and Worship

The bible states that its easier for a camel to go through the eye of a needle than for a rich man to enter the kingdom of God (**Matt. 19:23**). The process is actually hard if you had not gotten rich before. Your space, your heart, are crowded by your treasures. Therefore, the rich man would have to declutter the heart from the worship of money and stand in awe and worship God only.

The scripture is in no way saying that we should not be rich, but who do we choose to worship (to give our all, to pay obeisance to)? Who do we put first? There are many rich and wealthy in the earth, and also many aspiring millionaires, multimillionaires and billionaires. God's desire is for us to worship him, only and him only shall thou serve (**Matthew 4:10**).

Satan tempted Jesus in the wilderness and told him all the things he would have given unto him, if he would bow down and worship him. The senseless, ignorance of Satan couldn't even fathom that what he was promising Jesus was already owned by him (not just a fraction, but the entire universe). No wonder the scripture says, the Lord giveth and the Lord taketh away (**Job 1:21**), it all belongs to Him.

God is a jealous God, especially when his creations worship something else besides him. This is referring to the rich or the poor. (**Ex. 20:5**) God visits the iniquity of the fathers upon the third and fourth generations. Wealth brings comfort as well as destruction. It's truly how you operate before the God who allows you to gain it.

The only way you can serve and give true worship to God, is to remove the love of wealth out of your heart and let Jesus in. **Psalms 29:2 - "Worship the LORD in the beauty of holiness."** What does it profit a man to gain the whole world and lose his soul (**Mark 8:36**). We should pray that the rich and wealthy will worship and serve God only.

In reference to numerous churches that have a large number of members, obviously the larger the numbers would have reflected more wealth in place (if prosperity is managed). Smaller denominations would seemingly incur a smaller amount of riches (depending on the caliber of folks and the heart posture towards giving). In the business sector, it depends on the type of business that would profit more or less. **Romans 12:11** teaches us how not to become slothful in business. Note! That the church has a business side to it as well. Bottom line, it doesn't matter the amount or size.

When the world pounces upon the church in a taunting/judgmental manner concerning money, this would then be time for introspection, to see if our motives are pure and inclined concerning money matters. The world has a problem with the church being or becoming wealthy, and the church has a problem with the world being wealthy. We as citizens of Christ should know who our provider and supplier is. Competition should not be seen in us!

The truth is sometimes the world shows more solidarity in society extending their borders and going hard in accomplishing their goals. Jesus said in **Luke 16:18 - "for the children of this world are in their generation wiser than the children of light."** It means that children of the world are very shrewd in earning and storing wealth in the world for their happy life.

We agree with **Matthew 5:45**, that God rains on the just and the unjust. The Greek word for just is dikaios, meaning righteous (the distinguished hearers of the saints). The unjust would mean unrighteous. Both, God will bless, but only the just shall see his face.

> *I would therefore deem money*
> *to be that awesome tool*
> *that has fluidity to supply.*

The Presence of Money

The presence of money is rather delightful and welcoming as it is so needed for survival. God ensures that he balances out the spiritual with the natural. He is the provider that fulfills the financial needs on earth. I would therefore deem money as being that awesome tool that has fluidity to supply. Have you ever been in debt and somehow did not know what would happen to you or your family? The widow at Zarephath lost her husband, and he had debt, as well as two sons. Elisha came on the scene and challenged her regarding what she had left in her house. She had a few barrels, and she was told to go and borrow. The provision would not have manifested until she obeyed the prophet.

Can you imagine the exuberant praise she gave up to God. A huge burden was lifted off her shoulders. Her sons were spared from the creditors. She had oil to live off of, for the rest of her life. She became wealthy and the presence of money entered her life, home and family. How would you have felt in this case? It must have been a phenomenal experience for her life. Her husband was gone, but not God and not his presence, or his care (1 Kings 17:7-16).

Psalm 115:14 - "The Lord shall increase you more and more, you and your children."

We all have the need for the presence of money to fulfill our needs. Debt stared her in the face like many of us. It was nothing short of a miracle. There is also a miracle with your name on it. Owe no man nothing but to love them (**Romans 13:8**). Give to Ceasar what is for Ceasar and to God what is for God (**Mark 12:17**). The presence of money to clear your name is amazing. **Proverbs 22:1 - "A good name is rather to be chosen than great riches, and loving, favour rather than silver and gold."**

God releases the presence of money to bring comfort to those who are suffering and dying. It takes money to have shelters, for equipment and to pay doctors. It also runs earth's resources, and businesses. We must indeed appreciate God for the method and medium to which he uses to bless us and satisfy our needs. Hallelujah! We thank you and praise you, Lord!

We all should look into our lives to see and observe where our hearts are concerning money. Respect it! Be wise with it! Let it work for you. Adhere to good mannerism; for what we don't respect we chase away.

> “*I laid down the love for money,*
> *and watch God save,*
> *heal and deliver lives,*
> *while he blessed us.*

Money Magnet

As often as you can, declare these words. **"Thou shalt also decree a thing, and it shall be established unto thee: and the light shall shine upon thy ways." Job 22:28**

I am a money magnet; money is attracted to me.
I have hidden riches in secret places, even wealth from the seas.
I am pure in heart to master it and sanctified in thought to control it.
The heavens are opened up to me and wealth invites me.
Today I will not lack, God's store house is already packed.
My store basket will not go empty, because I am already wealthy.
Uncommon favors I receive, uncommon blessings have been released.
I am a lender, not a borrower. I am a giver, not a beggar.
I am a money magnet and always will be, and money you shall serve me,
in Jesus' name.

(It does not control my thoughts, I control it.)

Heavenly father, we repent before you. If we have put money before you, please forgive us. Jesus, we thank you for money, the currency that answers all things. It puts in place the provision of every financial need, of every human being on planet earth. Lord help us to attain the knowledge of how to utilize it. Give us wisdom to acquire the usage of money and to correctly dispense accordingly, in a powerful way. Correct us when we misappropriate the use of money. Teach us the mannerisms of money, how to truly respect your supply from heaven manifested on earth. Jesus, help us to put you first so that money will not be our Lord. Help us not to love it, but to avoid the root of evil from springing up within us. We thank you for the gift, the blessing and the signs that show us how you love and will always take care of us. We salute you, the God who supplies all our needs according to your riches in glory. Amen!

Biography

Apostle Maxine Gordon

Apostle Maxine Gordon, Peace Ambassador, UN, is the founder and CEO of "Heaven Blazing Earth Charity", which governs HBEMI's charity scholarship fund and the "Feed The 5,000" feeding programme. She is an idealistic person who cherishes goals, values, and dreams and also is a philanthropist at heart. With her giving, caring, donating, and seeking to look out for the welfare of persons, she has a strong passion for the poor and the needy and as such, birthed this HBEMI outreach ministry and charity.

Apostle Gordon is also the founder of "Woman Into Diamond", a platform enabling and impacting women to fulfill their God-given Purpose all over the Globe. She has also co-founded New Covenant Ministries International with her husband, Apostle Dr. Richardo Gordon, and is a supporting wife and a loving mother of four children: Shereca, Kurtlando, John, and Destinique, residing with her family in Highgate, St. Mary, Jamaica, W.I.

Being an accomplished Psalmist, Author, Song Writer, Recording Artiste, and Poet, Apostle Maxine Gordon has written over 600 songs and some of her notable and acclaimed works include the soul touching, "I Am A Winner" album and her literary breakthrough soul-searching study books, "Treasury Of A Lifetime" and "Pure Gems Of Glory". She is an International Business Woman and can be likened to the "Virtuous Woman" described in Proverbs 31.

Apostle Gordon has also been the recipient of Heavenly Downloads for course modules such as "The Glory of God", "The Fire of God", "The Call of God", "Understanding Prophetic Worship", "Angels, Healing & Miracles, Signs & Wonders", and "Advancing the Kingdom in Intercession". These courses take every participant on a life-changing journey in their relationship with God.

Though she is in full-time ministry, Apostle Gordon has traveled both nationally and internationally, ministering the Undiluted Word of God from the platform of Maxine Gordon Ministries. She has offered spiritual and emotional healing, as she guides persons in transforming their inner selves, and has also led many women into deeper, more fulfilling prayer and worshipful lives through her own epiphanies in the area.

Ministering with a strong prophetic mantle accompanied by deliverance, uncommon signs and wonders follow her ministry. She is known as a no-nonsense Preacher and a Holiness Prophet. Powerful, anointed trumpets resound from her belly, which creates spiritual atmospheres and mighty explosions, which often cause people to weep and shake heavily as she ministers.

Bibliography

Unless otherwise noted, all scripture is taken from King James Version (KJV) of the Bible (Public Domain in the USA).

Scripture quotations & marked bible versions of KJV, NLT, NKJV, ESV, NIV and taken from:

- King James Bible. (Public Domain in the USA)

- Holy Bible, New Living Translation, copyright © 1996, 2004, 2015 by Tyndale House Foundation. Used by permission of Tyndale House Publishers, Inc., Carol Stream, Illinois 60188. All rights reserved.

- The Holy Bible, New King James Version, Copyright © 1982 Thomas Nelson. All rights reserved.

- The ESV® Bible (The Holy Bible, English Standard Version®) copyright © 2001 by Crossway Bibles, a publishing ministry of Good News Publishers.

- Holy Bible, New International Version®, NIV® Copyright © 1973, 1978, 1984, 2011 by Biblica, Inc.® Used by permission. All rights reserved worldwide.

Word search, synonyms, and applicable definitions taken from:

- https://www.google.com/search?

- https://www.thesaurus.com/browse/
  ©2019 Dictionary.com, LLC

- Merriam-Webster Online
  (www.Merriam-Webster.com)

Epictetus quote:

- https://www.goodreads.com/quotes/71368-wealth-consists-not-in-having-great-possessions-but-in-having

Ayn Rand quote:

- https://www.goodreads.com/quotes/7215632-money-is-only-a-tool-it-will-take-you-wherever

BOOKS BY THE AUTHOR

PROPHETIC WORSHIP

Module Book

Course Objectives

(1) This Course will give a practical understanding of prophetic worship.

(2) students will receive biblical revelation coupled with personal experien show a pathway to prophetic worship.

(3) Students will be equipped with the knowledge of how to enter God's presence and lead others into it.

(4) Students will be given the practical tools of how to push in the glory an out divine provision both privately and publically.

(5) This study will provoke a craving for the manifest presence of God and more of the spirit .

(6) Students at the end of the course will be able to quantify what they lear through questions and answers.

THE GLORY OF GOD

Module Book

Course Objectives

(1) This Course was designed to take you into Dimension of God's Glory

(2) You will develop a hunger and passion to see God's Glory.

(3) You will be equipped on how to pull on God's Glory.

(4) You will receive revelation through God's Word.

(5) You will become a Glory Carrier.

(6) Glorious manifestation will become the order of your day.

LECTURER- Prophetess Maxine Gordon

PROPHETIC WORSHIP

MODULE COURSE

WORK BOOK

LECTURER: REV. MAXINE GORDON

MAXINE GORDON MINISTRIES

MAXINE GORDON MINISTRIES
MGM
MOTIVATE · GUIDE · MOBILIZE
The Fire of God
Module Course
Work Book
Lecturer Rev. Prophetess Maxine Gordon

MAXINE GORDON MINISTRIES
MGM
THE GLORY OF GOD
Mudule Workbook
Lecturer
Rev. Prophetess Maxine Gordon

PROPHETESS MAXINE GORDON

Pure Gems of Glory

First and foremost this book is a must read that will bring about great changes in your life. As the reader you will experience the hand of Jehovah God heavy upon you. It will promote divine transformation and turn around for you and angels of God that are assigned to you will begin to work on your behalf speedily and bring release as you receive tools that put angels to work. The principles found in this book are Biblical and will bring about sanctification, deliverance and healing even a new beginning in your life. As you read anticipate the blessing of the Lord from the crown of your head to the soles of your feet cause after you have suffered awhile you can only reflect His glory.

NOTES

NOTES

NOTES

NOTES

www.ingramcontent.com/pod-product-compliance
Lightning Source LLC
LaVergne TN
LVHW010617110826
845149LV00003B/950

* 9 7 9 8 9 9 8 8 5 1 6 4 3 *